Items should be returned on or before the date ___
not already requested by other borrowers m___
in writing or by telephone. To renew, please ___
barcode label. To renew online a PIN is requi___
at your local library.
Renew online @ **www.dublincitypubliclibrar**___
Fines charged for overdue items will include po___ ___.
Damage to or loss of items will be charged to th___ ___.

D0865945

**Leaeharlanna Poiblí
Chathair Bhaile Átha
Cliath**

Comhairle Cathrach
Bhaile Átha Cliath
Dublin City Council

Due Date	Due Date	Due Date

Published in 2018 by CICO Books
An imprint of Ryland Peters & Small Ltd
20–21 Jockey's Fields   341 E 116th St
London WC1R 4BW   New York, NY 10029

www.rylandpeters.com

10 9 8 7 6 5 4 3 2 1

Design © CICO Books 2018

For photography credits, see pages 127–128.

A CIP catalog record for this book is available
from the Library of Congress and the British
Library.

ISBN: 978-1-78249-589-5

Printed in China

Commissioning editor: Kristine Pidkameny
Senior editor: Carmel Edmonds
Designer: Paul Tilby
Art director: Sally Powell
Head of production: Patricia Harrington
Publishing manager: Penny Craig
Publisher: Cindy Richards

INTRODUCTION

Being in love is a magical feeling: Your heart misses a beat when that certain
someone walks into the room, and even on the dullest of days you feel as if the
sun is shining on everything you do. However, telling the object of your affections
how you feel is not always easy. So if you're racking your brains for a suitable
verse for a Valentine's Day card or to feature on wedding stationery, or simply
want to be inspired, then look no further.

Here you'll find memorable and heartfelt quotations, both ancient and
contemporary and from philosophers, novelists, poets, and other celebrated
figures. Whether you're suffering the bittersweet pangs of your first romance
or declaring your devotion to a lifelong partner, you'll discover words to suit all
moods and mind-sets.

SINCE LOVE GROWS
WITHIN YOU, SO
BEAUTY GROWS.
FOR LOVE IS
THE BEAUTY
OF THE SOUL.

St Augustine (354–430)

LOVE IS LIKE THE MEASLES; WE ALL HAVE TO GO THROUGH IT.

Jerome K. Jerome (1859–1927)

WE LOVE THE THINGS WE LOVE FOR WHAT THEY ARE.

Robert Frost (1874–1963)

TRUE LOVE COMES QUIETLY,
WITHOUT BANNERS
OR FLASHING LIGHTS.
IF YOU HEAR BELLS,
GET YOUR EARS CHECKED.

Erich Segal (1937–2010)

'TIS VERY MUCH LIKE LIGHT,
A THING THAT EVERYBODY
KNOWS, AND YET NONE CAN
TELL WHAT TO MAKE OF IT:
'TIS NOT MONEY, FORTUNE,
JOYNTURE, RAVING,
STABBING, HANGING,

ROMANCING, FLOUNCING, SWEARING, RAMPING, DESIRING, FIGHTING, DYING, THOUGH ALL THOSE HAVE BEEN, ARE, & STILL WILL BE MISTAKEN AND MISCALLED FOR IT.

Definition of love, from
The Ladies' Dictionary (1694)

LOVE IS THE WINE OF EXISTENCE.

Henry Ward Beecher
(1813–1887)

THAT LOVE IS ALL THERE IS, IS ALL WE KNOW OF LOVE.

Emily Dickinson
(1830–1886)

IF I MEET YOU SUDDENLY, I CAN'T SPEAK
—MY TONGUE IS BROKEN; A THIN FLAME
RUNS UNDER MY SKIN; SEEING NOTHING,
HEARING ONLY MY OWN EARS DRUMMING,
I DRIP WITH SWEAT; TREMBLING SHAKES MY
BODY AND I TURN PALER THAN DRY GRASS.
AT SUCH TIMES DEATH ISN'T FAR FROM ME.

Sappho (6th century BCE)

WHAT LOVE IS, IF THOU WOULDST BE TAUGHT,
THE HEART MUST TEACH ALONE—
TWO SOULS WITH BUT A SINGLE THOUGHT,
TWO HEARTS THAT BEAT AS ONE.

Friedrich Halm (1806–1871)

LOVE IS
A BINDING FORCE,
BY WHICH ANOTHER
IS JOINED TO ME &
CHERISHED
BY MYSELF.

Thomas Aquinas (c. 1225–1274)

O, LOVE, LOVE, LOVE!
LOVE IS LIKE A DIZZINESS;
IT WINNA [WILL NOT] LET A POOR BODY
GANG [GO] ABOUT HIS BIZINESS!

James Hogg (1770–1835)

LOVE LOOKS
NOT WITH
THE EYES,
BUT WITH
THE MIND:
AND THEREFORE
IS WING'D
CUPID
PAINTED
BLIND.

William Shakespeare
(1564–1616)

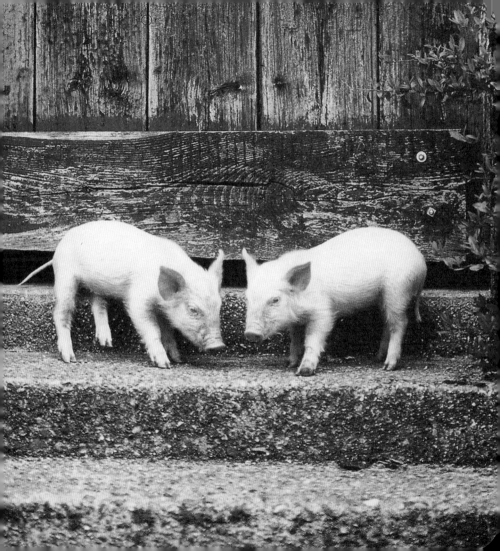

THE WINDS WERE WARM ABOUT US,
THE WHOLE EARTH SEEMED
THE WEALTHIER FOR OUR LOVE.

Harriet Prescott Spofford (1835–1921)

WE'VE GOT THIS GIFT OF LOVE,
BUT LOVE IS LIKE A PRECIOUS PLANT.
YOU CAN'T JUST ACCEPT IT AND LEAVE IT
IN THE CUPBOARD OR JUST THINK IT'S
GOING TO GET ON BY ITSELF.
YOU'VE GOT TO KEEP WATERING IT.
YOU'VE GOT TO REALLY LOOK AFTER
IT AND NURTURE IT.

John Lennon (1940–1980)

NOTHING TAKES THE TASTE OUT OF PEANUT BUTTER QUITE LIKE UNREQUITED LOVE.

Charlie Brown in "Peanuts" comic strip, created by Charles M. Schultz

**LOVE WING'D MY HOPES
AND TAUGHT ME HOW TO FLY.**

Anonymous

DOUBT THOU THE STARS ARE FIRE,
DOUBT THAT THE SUN DOTH MOVE,
DOUBT TRUTH TO BE A LIAR,
BUT NEVER DOUBT I LOVE.

William Shakespeare (1564–1616)

LOVE CONQUERS
ALL THINGS:
LET US, TOO,
GIVE IN
TO LOVE

Virgil (70–19 BCE)

PEOPLE WHO ARE NOT IN LOVE FAIL TO UNDERSTAND HOW AN INTELLIGENT MAN CAN SUFFER BECAUSE OF A VERY ORDINARY WOMAN. THIS IS LIKE BEING SURPRISED THAT ANYONE SHOULD BE STRICKEN WITH CHOLERA BECAUSE OF A CREATURE SO INSIGNIFICANT AS THE COMMON BACILLUS.

Marcel Proust (1871–1922)

IF I LOVED YOU LESS, I MIGHT BE ABLE TO TALK ABOUT IT MORE

Jane Austen (1775–1817)

LOVE WILL DRAW AN ELEPHANT THROUGH A KEY-HOLE.

Samuel Richardson
(1689–1761)

AS SOON GO KINDLE FIRE
WITH SNOW, AS SEEK
TO QUENCH THE FIRE OF
LOVE WITH WORDS.

William Shakespeare (1564–1616)

LIFE WITHOUT LOVE IS LIKE A TREE WITHOUT BLOSSOMS OR FRUIT.

Kahlil Gibran (1883–1931)

DO NOT SMILE TO YOURSELF
LIKE A GREEN MOUNTAIN
WITH A CLOUD DRIFTING ACROSS IT.
PEOPLE WILL KNOW WE ARE IN LOVE.

Otomo no Sakanoe no Iratsume (c. 700–750)

IF GRASS CAN GROW THROUGH CEMENT, LOVE CAN FIND YOU AT EVERY TIME IN YOUR LIFE.

Cher (1946–)

MY BOUNTY IS AS BOUNDLESS AS THE SEA,
MY LOVE AS DEEP. THE MORE I GIVE TO THEE
THE MORE I HAVE, FOR BOTH ARE INFINITE.

William Shakespeare (1564–1616)

TO LOVE SOMEONE DEEPLY GIVES YOU STRENGTH. BEING LOVED BY SOMEONE DEEPLY GIVES YOU COURAGE.

Lao Tzu

(c. 604–531 BCE)

THOU ART MY LIFE, MY LOVE, MY HEART,
THE VERY EYES OF ME:
AND HAST COMMAND OF EVERY PART
TO LIVE AND DIE FOR THEE.

Robert Herrick (1591–1674)

AT THE TOUCH OF LOVE EVERYONE BECOMES A POET.

Plato (c. 427–347 BCE)

HOW DO I LOVE THEE?
LET ME COUNT THE WAYS.
I LOVE THEE TO THE
DEPTH AND BREADTH AND HEIGHT
MY SOUL CAN REACH.

Elizabeth Barrett Browning (1806–1861)

HERE ARE FRUITS, FLOWERS, LEAVES, AND BRANCHES, AND HERE IS MY HEART WHICH BEATS ONLY FOR YOU.

Paul Verlaine (1844–1896)

YOU ARE MY
HEART,
MY LIFE,
MY ONE
AND ONLY
THOUGHT.

Sir Arthur Conan Doyle
(1859–1930)

I LOVE YOU
AS NEW ENGLANDERS
LOVE PIE.

Don Marquis (1878–1937)

I, MY SWEET & DARLING ONE,
WITH WHOM I WOULD SPEAK HONEY
—YOUTH, I AM IN LOVE WITH YOU!

Kubatum
(Sumerian priestess, c. 2032 BCE)

WHATEVER OUR SOULS ARE MADE OF, HIS & MINE ARE THE SAME.

Emily Brontë (1818–1848)

EROS
HAS SHAKEN
MY THOUGHTS, LIKE
A WIND AMONG
HIGHLAND OAKS.

Sappho
(6th century BCE)

I CAN NO LONGER THINK
OF ANYTHING BUT YOU.
IN SPITE OF MYSELF, MY
IMAGINATION CARRIES ME
TO YOU. I GRASP YOU,
I KISS YOU, I CARESS YOU,
A THOUSAND OF THE MOST
AMOROUS CARESSES
TAKE POSSESSION OF ME.

Honoré de Balzac (1799–1850)

DESTINY, WITH ITS MYSTERIOUS
AND FATAL PATIENCE, SLOWLY
DREW TOGETHER THESE TWO
BEINGS, ALL CHARGED AND ALL
LANGUISHING WITH THE STORMY
ELECTRICITY OF PASSION,
THESE TWO SOULS WHICH WERE
LADEN WITH LOVE AS TWO
CLOUDS ARE LADEN WITH
LIGHTNING, AND WHICH
WERE BOUND TO OVERFLOW
AND MINGLE IN A LOOK LIKE THE
CLOUDS IN A FLASH OF FIRE.

Victor Hugo (1802–1885)

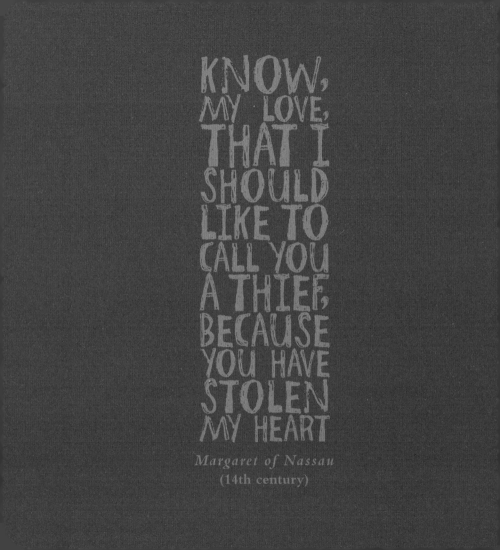

KNOW,
MY LOVE,
THAT I
SHOULD
LIKE TO
CALL YOU
A THIEF,
BECAUSE
YOU HAVE
STOLEN
MY HEART

Margaret of Nassau
(14th century)

**WHEN MY SELF IS NOT WITH YOU,
IT IS NOWHERE.**

Héloise (c. 1098–1164)

I LOVE THEE—I LOVE THEE,
'TIS ALL THAT I CAN SAY;—
IT IS MY VISION IN THE NIGHT,
MY DREAMING IN THE DAY.

Thomas Hood (1799–1845)

THERE IS A LADY SWEET AND KIND,
WAS NEVER FACE SO PLEASED MY MIND;
I DID BUT SEE HER PASSING BY,
AND YET I LOVE HER TIL I DIE.

Anonymous

O MY LUVE'S LIKE A RED, RED ROSE, THAT'S NEWLY SPRUNG IN JUNE

Robert Burns (1759–1796)

AH, HOW SWEET IT IS TO LOVE!

AH, HOW GAY IS YOUNG DESIRE!

AND WHAT PLEASING PAINS WE PROVE

WHEN WE FIRST APPROACH LOVE'S FIRE!

PAINS OF LOVE BE SWEETER FAR

THAN ALL OTHER PLEASURES ARE.

John Dryden (1631–1700)

**AT ONE GLANCE
I LOVE YOU
WITH A
THOUSAND HEARTS**

Mihri Hatun
(?–1506)

THE MAGIC OF FIRST LOVE IS OUR IGNORANCE THAT IT CAN EVER END.

Benjamin Disraeli (1804–1881)

**BUT TO SEE HER,
WAS TO LOVE HER;
LOVE BUT HER,
AND LOVE FOR EVER.**

Robert Burns (1759–1796)

A KISS IS A LOVELY TRICK DESIGNED
BY NATURE TO STOP SPEECH WHEN WORDS
BECOME SUPERFLUOUS.

Ingrid Bergman (1915–1982)

HE WALKED DOWN,
FOR A LONG WHILE
AVOIDING LOOKING AT HER
AS AT THE SUN,
BUT SEEING HER,
AS ONE DOES THE SUN,
WITHOUT LOOKING.

Leo Tolstoy (1828–1910)

HOW ON EARTH ARE YOU EVER
GOING TO EXPLAIN IN TERMS OF
CHEMISTRY & PHYSICS SO IMPORTANT
A BIOLOGICAL PHENOMENON
AS FIRST LOVE?

Albert Einstein (1879–1955)

UNTIL THEN, MIO DOLCE AMOR,

A THOUSAND KISSES;

BUT GIVE ME NONE IN RETURN,

FOR THEY SET MY BLOOD ON FIRE.

Napoleon Bonaparte (1769–1821)

SOUL MEETS SOUL ON LOVERS' LIPS

Percy Bysshe Shelley
(1792–1822)

FRIENDS, YOU ARE LUCKY YOU
CAN TALK ABOUT WHAT YOU DID
AS LOVERS: THE TRICKS, LAUGHTER,
THE WORDS, THE ECSTASY.
AFTER MY DARLING PUT HIS HAND
ON THE KNOT OF MY DRESS,
I SWEAR I REMEMBER NOTHING.

Vidya (fl. c. 700–1050)

KISSING IS LIKE DRINKING SALTED WATER. YOU DRINK, AND YOUR THIRST INCREASES.

Chinese proverb

ONE REGRET, DEAR WORLD,
THAT I AM DETERMINED
NOT TO HAVE WHEN I LIE ON
MY DEATHBED IS THAT I DID
NOT KISS YOU ENOUGH.

Hafiz of Persia (1321–1389)

LET HIM KISS ME WITH THE KISSES
OF HIS MOUTH! FOR YOUR LOVE
IS BETTER THAN WINE.

Bible: Song of Solomon 1:2.

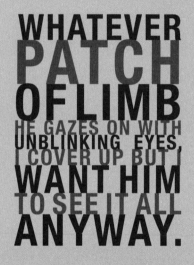

WHATEVER PATCH OF LIMB HE GAZES ON WITH UNBLINKING EYES, I COVER UP BUT I **WANT HIM** TO SEE IT ALL **ANYWAY.**

Hla Stavhana
(South Indian king, c. 50 CE)

COMING TO KISS HER LIPS,
(SUCH GRACE I FOUND)
MESEEM'D, I SMELT A GARDEN
OF SWEET FLOWERS.

Edmund Spenser (c.1552–1599)

ONCE HE DREW
WITH ONE
LONG KISS
MY WHOLE SOUL
THROUGH MY LIPS,
AS SUNLIGHT
DRINKETH DEW.

Alfred, Lord Tennyson
(1809–1892)

WHERE BOTH DELIBERATE, THE LOVE IS SLIGHT, WHO EVER LOVED, THAT LOVED NOT AT FIRST SIGHT?

Christopher Marlowe
(1564–1593)

MY SWEET ONE, WASH ME WITH HONEY—
IN THE BED THAT IS FILLED WITH HONEY,
LET US ENJOY OUR LOVE.
LION, LET ME GIVE YOU MY CARESSES,
MY SWEET ONE, AWASH ME WITH HONEY.

Kubatum (Sumerian priestess, c. 2032 BCE)

STAY, O SWEET AND DO NOT RISE!
THE LIGHT THAT SHINES COMES FROM THINE EYES;
THE DAY BREAKS NOT: IT IS MY HEART,
BECAUSE THAT YOU & I MUST PART.
STAY! OR ELSE MY JOYS WILL DIE AND PERISH
IN THEIR INFANCY.

John Donne (1573–1631)

THE GIVING OF LOVE IS AN EDUCATION IN ITSELF.

Eleanor Roosevelt (1884–1962)

I PAY VERY LITTLE REGARD TO WHAT
ANY YOUNG PERSON SAYS ON THE SUBJECT
OF MARRIAGE. IF THEY PROFESS
A DISINCLINATION FOR IT,
I ONLY SET IT DOWN THAT THEY HAVE
NOT YET SEEN THE RIGHT PERSON.

Jane Austen (1775–1817)

I HAVE FOR THE FIRST TIME FOUND WHAT I CAN TRULY LOVE — I HAVE FOUND YOU. YOU ARE MY SYMPATHY — MY BETTER SELF — MY GOOD ANGEL. I AM BOUND TO YOU WITH A STRONG ATTACHMENT. I THINK YOU GOOD, GIFTED, LOVELY: A

FERVENT, A SOLEMN PASSION IS CONCEIVED IN MY HEART; IT LEANS TO YOU, DRAWS YOU TO MY CENTRE AND SPRINGS OF LIFE, WRAPS MY EXISTENCE ABOUT YOU, AND, KINDLING IN PURE, POWERFUL FLAME, FUSES YOU AND ME IN ONE.

Charlotte Brontë (1816–1855)

COME LIVE WITH ME AND
BE MY LOVE, AND WE WILL
ALL THE PLEASURES PROVE
THAT HILLS AND VALLEYS,
DALE AND FIELD, AND ALL THE
CRAGGY MOUNTAINS YIELD.

Christopher Marlowe (1564–1593)

**ONE WORD FREES US OF ALL
THE WEIGHT AND PAIN OF LIFE:
THAT WORD IS LOVE.**

Sophocles (c. 496–406 BCE)

ALL, EVERYTHING THAT I UNDERSTAND,
I UNDERSTAND ONLY BECAUSE I LOVE.

Victor Hugo (1802–1885)

I WILL COVER YOU WITH LOVE WHEN
NEXT I SEE YOU, WITH CARESSES, WITH ECSTASY.
I WANT TO GORGE YOU WITH ALL THE JOYS
OF THE FLESH, SO THAT YOU FAINT AND DIE.
I WANT YOU TO BE AMAZED BY ME, AND TO
CONFESS TO YOURSELF THAT YOU HAD NEVER
EVEN DREAMED OF SUCH TRANSPORTS ... WHEN
YOU ARE OLD, I WANT YOU TO RECALL THOSE FEW
HOURS, I WANT YOUR DRY BONES TO QUIVER
WITH JOY WHEN YOU THINK OF THEM.

Gustave Flaubert (1821–1880)

**MANY WATERS CANNOT QUENCH LOVE,
NEITHER CAN FLOODS DROWN IT.**

Bible: Song of Solomon, 8:7

WHAT GREATER THING IS THERE FOR
TWO HUMAN SOULS, THAN TO FEEL
THAT THEY ARE JOINED FOR LIFE—TO
STRENGTHEN EACH OTHER IN ALL LABOUR,
TO REST ON EACH OTHER IN ALL
SORROW, TO MINISTER TO EACH OTHER
IN ALL PAIN, TO BE ONE WITH EACH
OTHER IN SILENT UNSPEAKABLE MEMORIES
AT THE MOMENT OF THE LAST PARTING?

George Eliot (1819–1880)

**WE LOVED WITH A LOVE
THAT WAS MORE THAN LOVE.**

Edgar Allen Poe (1809–1849)

**GROW OLD ALONG WITH ME!
THE BEST IS YET TO BE.**

Robert Browning (1882–1889)

I LOVED HER AGAINST REASON,
AGAINST PROMISE, AGAINST PEACE,
AGAINST HOPE, AGAINST HAPPINESS,
AGAINST ALL DISCOURAGEMENT
THAT COULD BE.

Charles Dickens (1812–1870)

I KNOW BY EXPERIENCE
THAT THE POETS ARE RIGHT:
LOVE IS ETERNAL.

E M Forster (1879–1970)

IT HAS MADE ME BETTER,
LOVING YOU;
IT HAS MADE ME WISER AND
EASIER AND BRIGHTER
AND NICER AND EVEN STRONGER.

Henry James (1843–1916)

**THERE WE TWO, CONTENT,
HAPPY IN BEING TOGETHER,
SPEAKING LITTLE,
PERHAPS NOT A WORD.**

Walt Whitman (1819–1892)

NO, THERE'S
NOTHING
HALF SO
SWEET
IN LIFE AS
LOVE'S
YOUNG
DREAM.

Thomas Moore
(1779–1852)

I WISH I HAD THE GIFT OF
MAKING RHYMES, FOR METHINKS
THERE IS POETRY IN MY
HEAD AND HEART SINCE
I HAVE BEEN IN LOVE WITH YOU.

Nathaniel Hawthorne (1804–1864)

GIVE ME A KISS, AND TO THAT
KISS A SCORE; THEN TO THAT
TWENTY, ADD A HUNDRED
MORE; A THOUSAND TO THAT
HUNDRED; SO KISS ON,

TO MAKE THAT THOUSAND UP

A MILLION; TREBLE THAT

MILLION, AND WHEN THAT IS

DONE, LET'S KISS AFRESH,

AS WHEN WE FIRST BEGUN.

Robert Herrick (1592–1674)

**LOVE IS PATIENT;
LOVE IS KIND;
LOVE IS NOT ENVIOUS
OR BOASTFUL
OR ARROGANT
OR RUDE.**

Bible: 1 Corinthians, 13:1

I GIVE MYSELF TO YOU, BELOVED!

Amy Lowell (1874–1926)

ONCE THE REALIZATION IS ACCEPTED THAT EVEN BETWEEN THE CLOSEST HUMAN BEINGS INFINITE DISTANCES CONTINUE TO EXIST, A WONDERFUL LIVING SIDE BY SIDE CAN GROW UP, IF THEY SUCCEED IN LOVING THE DISTANCE BETWEEN THEM WHICH MAKES IT POSSIBLE FOR EACH TO SEE THE OTHER WHOLE AND AGAINST A WIDE SKY!

Rainer Maria Rilke (1875–1926)

**IS IT POSSIBLE
THAT LOVE SHOULD
OF A SUDDEN
TAKE SUCH HOLD?**

William Shakespeare
(1564–1616)

PHOTOGRAPHY CREDITS

Front cover: © Getty/Cyndi Monaghan

Back cover: © Getty/Kazuo Yasuoka/EyeEm

Page 1: www.barefoot-glamping.co.uk.
ph Debi Treloar

Page 2: *ph* Polly Wreford

Page 5: www.sarah-janedownthelane.blogspot.com. *ph* Debi Treloar

Page 6: *ph* Kate Whitaker

Page 9: Ritva Puotila's summerhome in Finland.
ph Paul Ryan

Page 13: *ph* Alan Williams

Page 15: Imogen Chappel's home in Suffolk.
ph Debi Treloar

Page 17: www.vintage-events.com. *ph* Debi Treloar

Page 18: Justin & Jenny Green, owners of Ballyvolane House.
ph James Fennell

Page 20: www.sarah-janedownthelane.blogspot.com. *ph* Debi Treloar

Page 23: *ph* Alan Williams

Page 25: *ph* Martin Brigdale

Page 26: www.davidaustinroses.com.
ph Debi Treloar

Page 29: *ph* Martin Norris

Page 30: *ph* Mark Scott

Page 32: *ph* Polly Wreford

Page 35: *ph* Richard Jung

Page 37: *ph* Henry Bourne

Page 38: *ph* Kim Lightbody

Page 39: *ph* Ian Wallace

Page 41: *ph* Michelle Garrett

Pages 42–43: *ph* Earl Carter

Page 44: *ph* Melanie Eclare